3co/#14gr · N-œ
L23

Bygone Bradford

D1597128

Bygone Bradford

The 'Lost World' of J. B. Priestley

by

Gary Firth

Dalesman Books
1986

The Dalesman Publishing Company Ltd.,
Clapham, Lancaster, LA2 8EB

First Published 1986

© Text and captions, Gary Firth 1986

© Quotations, Estate of J. B. Priestley 1986

Cover design by Ruth Owers

ISBN: 0 85206 878 6

Printed by Swannack Brown & Co. Ltd., Hull, England.

Introduction

THIS publication attempts to provide a few chance glimpses of Bradford life in the years shortly before the First World War. Through the written words of a great writer, and by and large, the photographic plates of a relatively unknown amateur photographer the flavour and character of Edwardian Bradford as a vigorous go-ahead provincial city shows through.

Occasionally the written word complements the photograph perfectly and vice versa. Then, it seems more than a coincidence that these two young men, Jack Priestley and Christopher Pratt, should be contemporaries at the same school in the same city. Bradford's cultural influences were at work on them both and, conversely, their creative genius reflects the very culture which was moulding them. Together, I trust they will bring the reader an enjoyment, and not a little understanding, of what Priestley once described as his 'lost world'.

John Boynton Priestley and Christopher Pratt were both born into the Bradford of the 1890s, a provincial urban community rich in cultural as well as economic terms. The nineteenth century was the age of the great provincial towns and Priestley's Bradford was one of the most notable northern cities. By the time he left it in 1914 Bradford was beginning to lose some of its influence and importance.

It has been described as the classic Victorian city growing from a small market town in 1801 to the seventh largest city in Britain fifty years later. By 1881 the consistently upward trend of Bradford's population growth had faltered and thereafter population increase was maintained by the extension of its municipal boundaries into Allerton, Heaton and Tyersal. The traditional heartland of industrial Bradford was vacated by the population as thousands of artisan and middle-class families fled like lemmings to the suburbs of Bradford Moor, Heaton and Allerton. The facilitator of this migration was the introduction of the horse bus and, later, tram cars driven by steam (1882) and by electricity from 1898.

It was in one of Bradford's more salubrious suburbs, Manningham, that Jack Priestley was born, September 13, 1894, at 34 Mannheim Road, off Toller Lane. His parents were from different social and cultural backgrounds. His mother was a mill girl and died early in his life. Jonathan Priestley, his father, came from an altogether different environment, belonging to the respectable, upwardly mobile ranks of the working class. J. B. Priestley's grandfather was an overlooker employed in one of Bradford's many mills and managed to save enough money to send his son to teacher training college. Jonathan Priestley taught for some years at Belle

in Drawing

23. August. 1894.
    Registration Examined 1.
        Walter Ackroyd.

Aug 28   Mr Shepherdson absent to-day through
          illness
Sept 11th Mr Priestley absent this afternoon

          Report of H. M. Inspector . 1893-4.
          "This School is ably conducted, and
          the quality of the elementary work
          is thoroughly good, being accurate
          and intelligent throughout. The
          singing and music are excellent; of

Jonathan Priestley with some of his pupils from Green Lane school
(top); Belle Vue School logbook showing Jonathan Priestley's absence
at the time of the birth of his son, Jack (bottom).

34, Mannheim Road, birthplace of J. B. Priestley.

Vue school and was later to become headmaster of a large new elementary school at Green Lane, Bradford. Priestley Senior was a socialist of the traditional kind shaped more by Wesley and William Morris than by the doctrinaire socialism of Karl Marx.

In the year before J. B. Priestley's birth Bradford had been the venue of the inaugural conference of the Independent Labour Party. At its Labour Institute in Peckover Street, Bradford's Labour Union had made a major contribution to the founding of this national party for working men and women. Priestley senior, as a

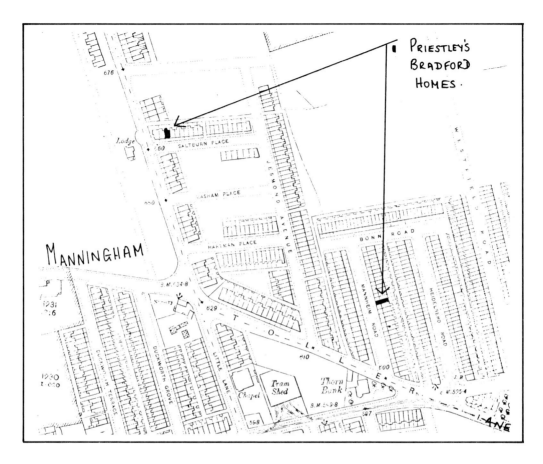

Jack Priestley's Bradford homes.
Opposite: 5, Saltburn Place. The attic where Priestley showed an early genius for creative writing.

socialist and a big N.U.T. man, doubtless contributed to this success. His son, though never a member of the Labour Party, sympathised with that tradition of liberal socialism and social justice which prevailed before the First World War. In his literary works he mourned its passing and would have no truck with the anaemic doctrinaire socialism which replaced it. J. B. Priestley was the kind of socialist who wore his socialism on his sleeve not in his head. If only there were more like him today.

> 'There was nothing of the bitter rebel about my uncle, and no revolution could ever have been of his making, but nevertheless he held strong progressive views, was always ready to defend them, and often surprised me by showing much skill

School				
Surname *Priestley*	Christian Names *Jack*			Sex *male*
Name of Father or Guardian *Jonathan*	Postal Address *5 Saltburn Place, Bradford*			

	8. Place of Residence.	9. Occupation of Father.	10. Place or places of previous education during the
1. Date of Birth. Day *13* Month *9* Year *94*	County Borough or County *Bradford*	*School master*	*Bradford, Whitby farm*
2. Date of Admission. Day *27* Month *8* Year *07*	and (a) Borough or (b) Urban District or (c) Rural Parish		*Belle Vue Boys' Prep*
3. Date of Leaving. Day *31* Month *7* Year *10*	11. Particulars of any exemption from Tuition fees.		12. Particulars of any Public Examinations passed or Certificates in the School, with dates.
4. Position on Admission. *IH*	(a) *Total exemption.* Granted from (Date). *Aug 1903*	(b) *Partial exemption.* Granted from (Date).	
5. Position on Leaving. *Form 5*	Granted by (Body awarding). *Bradford E.A.*	Granted by (Body awarding).	
6. Boarder or Day-Scholar. *Day*		Annual Amount	
7. Terms kept.	Tenable for *2 yrs + renewable*	Tenable for	
Autumn Spring Summer *06 06 06* *07 07 07* *08 08 08* *09 09 09*	14. Scholarships or Exhibitions for further education.	15. Place of further education.	16. Occupation taken up after leaving. *Shipping House Clerk.*

Admission register at Belle Vue school showing Priestley's admission to the school in 1907 (above); Belle Vue School logbook showing the school's status as a Higher Grade school (opposite top); J. B. Priestley's first school at Whetley Lane (opposite bottom).

and tenacity in argument. He still lived in that early optimistic Labour atmosphere, before anybody had sold out and before the party machinery had grown too elaborate.'

Bright Day (1946)

'Bright Day' published in 1946 was the most personal of Priestley's novels, written out of the personal crisis of the middle-aged writer taking stock, going back to his 'roots' once more and being inspired by the somewhat Arcadian belief in that pre-1914 world of industrial West Yorkshire. Priestley often gave the impression that life was better before 1914 and was never quite as good thereafter. The book is technically very sound, Priestley merging, with much subtlety, pre-1914 Yorkshire (Bruddersford) with post-1945 England. The magical, comfortable world of pre-1914 Bruddersford is symbolised by the Arlingtons, a middle class, culturally-aware

Mr Priestley has been appointed Head of the Evening School. He leaves on Friday

Sept 5. New No. for School of Science 5351 received

" Mr Marsden returned this afternoon after 2½ days illness.

School of Science report from Board of Education 1901 — 1902

This is an excellent type of a Higher Grade School. The instruction throughout is of a sound practical character, well adapted to the requirements of the Students. The

family whose world is threatened and finally ended by international war and economic slump.

In 1904 the Priestley family moved just round the corner to the more middle class environment of 5, Saltburn Place, Manningham, which

> 'had a kitchen where we ate when we were by ourselves; a front room where we ate when we had company; a smaller and gloomier back room . . . a bathroom on the half landing, two bedrooms and two attics. The front attic was my bedroom from the first and afterwards . . . my "den". The house, solidly built of stone cost about £550.'

The Edwardians (1970)

At Saltburn Place the houseowners had to pay for the upkeep of the street which offered a short cut for local wagon drivers. Jonathan Priestley was quick to defend his rights.

> 'no petty tyrants in a collectivist state could have pushed him around . . . he was always jumping up from the dinner table to dash out and remonstrate with invading lorry drivers'.

The Listener, July 1959.

Christopher Pratt at Highcliffe House in 1904.

In those years before the First World War, socialist pioneers were on the move in Bradford, particularly in the field of educational welfare. The medical supervision of Bradford schoolchildren began in 1893 and the first school baths were opened at Wapping six years later. Special educational facilities for the physically handicapped and educationally sub-normal were introduced by Bradford Corporation in the first decade of the twentieth century and in 1907 the first ever school meals service was run from Jonathan Priestley's school at Green Lane.

Meanwhile the young Priestley attended Whetley Lane Primary School where he gained a scholarship to Belle Vue High School where his father had recently taught. Belle Vue school was one of half a dozen Higher Grade schools which had developed quite naturally out of Bradford's very successful School Board system. They were extensions of the elementary schools and provided a ladder for working class children to reach the rarefied atmosphere of higher education at the universities. In effect, they were a nascent public secondary school sector which threatened Bradford's out of date voluntary denominational schools, both Anglican and Nonconformist alike. Another pupil at Belle Vue School at the turn of the century was Christopher Pratt, son of Thomas Pratt and grandson of Christopher Pratt senior who had founded a successful furniture manufacturing business in North Parade, Bradford in 1845. Born at Hallfield Road, young Christopher was taken by his parents to live in the nearby moorland village of Baildon where he was introduced to his lifelong fascination with the flora and fauna of the West Yorkshire countryside. Back in Bradford at Highcliffe House, Undercliffe, Christopher cultivated his hobby of wildlife photography building hides and specialist cages. His photographic records of West Yorkshire bird and insect life won him several photographic competitions. He was much inspired by the pioneering wildlife photography of Richard and Cherry Kearton of Swaledale. Using a quarter plate camera and tripod with bellows and a silent shutter the young man built up a precious collection of glass negatives. Christopher Pratt's parents and grandparents were lifelong Methodists who worshipped at Eastbrook Chapel and, in 1904, following the opening of Eastbrook Hall the Methodists began a massive campaign of missionary work around Bradford. Young Pratt's contribution was to illustrate this public-relations exercise, with a series of photographs of Bradford life in 1904. Many of the photographs in this book have been taken from Christopher Pratt's unique collection of glass negatives of Edwardian Bradford. They provide a perfect visual complement to the written word of his more famous school contemporary.

Jack Priestley, like Christopher Pratt, also attended – albeit reluctantly – a Nonconformist chapel. Bradford had long held a tradition of Nonconformity; the 1851 Religious Census showed that a majority of working people in the town attended neither church nor chapel but sixty per cent of those who did were dissenters of one kind or another and were doubtless at the forefront of the dissenters' campaign to disestablish the Anglican church in the 1870s. However, when Jack Priestley was a lad dissent was on the retreat in Bradford. The congregations of many denominations dwindled in the face of middle class migration to the suburbs, a resurgence of Anglicanism and the alternative attractions of mass leisure activities, particularly cycling, pedestrianism and football. The latter was popularised by the founding of Bradford City Football Club in 1903 at Valley Parade. Their local following was swelled in 1911 when they were successful in the final of the English Cup.

In that year John Boynton Priestley, with no natural academic inclinations, was ready to leave school, secretly coveting a career in writing. In fact, his father found him a job as a junior clerk in the wool sorting firm of Messrs. Helm and Company, whose premises were in the Swan Arcade, Market Street. The work was dull and he detested the job. The wool trade was an inevitable occupation for many young men in Bradford at that time. Bradford, after all, was the world centre of worsted cloth production and since the 1850s had been a veritable Worstedopolis. In 1911 textiles was the largest source of employment in the city employing 27,393 men and 34,232 women.

The industry continued to be run by small family firms, although dominated by the large business empires like those of S. C. Lister, Titus Salt, Daniel Illingworth, Christopher Waud and H. W. Ripley. Their fortunes had been made in the middle of the nineteenth century. But after 1874 the vagaries of the wool trade prevented the growth of similar industrial empires. It was a period of economic uncertainty; of falling prices and profits and of receding markets. This 'relative depression' led to major structural changes in the industry. As other countries in the world industrialised and developed their production of cloth, Bradford manufacturers supplied them with yarn for their weaving sheds and, later, with combed tops for their spinning frames.

Despite this trend of its manufacturers moving down the production cycle, Bradford was still the King of West Riding textile communities.

> 'Wherever good cloth is valued there Bradford is known. Bradford has never merely dealt with this place and that, but had dealt with the whole wide world, putting a best coat and waistcoat on the planet itself...'
>
> *Heaton Review*, Vol.4, 1931.

Priestley's job at Helm & Company put him in touch with Bradford's cosmopolitanism as he opened endless blue wrapped samples of wool and hair from all parts of the globe.

> ' "It's camel 'air, that is – an' mucky stuff it is an' all." He pointed to the dust and bits of dried dung. "An' that's some from some desert, that is, so take a good look at it. I expect yer think we know nowt 'ere in Bruddersford, but let me tell yer, lad, we go out to the ends o' the earth, an' ends o' the earth come 'ere an' all." '
>
> *Bright Day* (1946)

However, in the front attic of 5, Saltburn Place, J. B. Priestley could turn his back on the wool trade and turn his mind to what he liked doing best, creative writing.

> 'Once I had climbed those stairs and closed the door behind me I was no longer a junior wool clerk, I was a writer – poet, story teller, humourist, commentator and social philosopher, at least in my own estimation...'

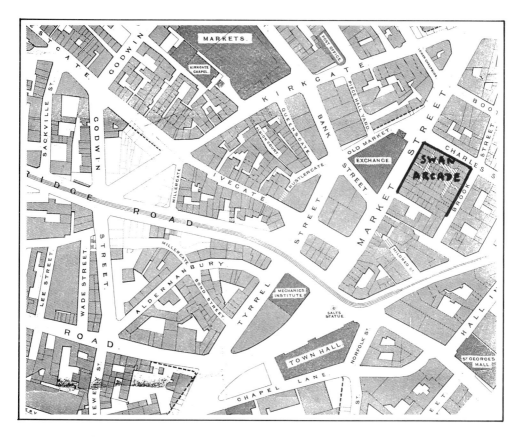

Location of Swan Arcade, opposite the Wool Exchange in Market Street.

In January 1913 he was given a column in the Bradford Labour weekly journal, the *Bradford Pioneer*, though he was never a member of the Labour Party himself, his 'Round the Hearth' column commented upon Bradford's cultural scene with notices about concerts, drama, books and the local variety theatre. And what a rich cultural setting Bradford held for him in those pre-war days!

When he was almost seventy years of age, in 1965, Priestley wrote a novel 'Lost Empires' about the early music and variety halls. This symbolic work provides a balanced picture of both the vibrant and gloomy sides of variety theatre. It is in turn, funny, sad and nostalgic; a melange of both gloom and joy. Like 'Bright Day' it draws very much on Priestley's experiences in Bradford before 1914 when he was a frequent visitor to the Palace Theatre in Manchester Road and the Empire, at the bottom of Great Horton Road. He sat there, night after night enjoying comic turns like Little Tich and Grock, but despising 'star' male-impersonators like Hetty King who 'bored the hell' out of Priestley.

A tram ride into the city from his home put him in touch with the best of classical music of the Halle subscription concerts at St. George's Hall, as well as the town's own symphony orchestra; with the Arts Club, Playgoers Society; with the cafe life at Lyons in Market Street, and particularly with the fourpenny balcony and knockabout comedians at the Empire Music Hall. If he took the same tram in the opposite direction he could soon find himself on the edge of the moors at Bingley and Cottingley.

> 'Thus Bradford is a city entirely without charm, though not altogether ugly, and its industry is a black business... but it has the good fortune to be on the edge of some of the most enchanted country in England. A sharp walk of less than an hour from more than one tram terminus will bring you to the moors, wild virgin highland, and every mill and warehouse will be out of sight and the whole city forgotten. However poor you are in Bradford, you need never be walled in, bricked up, as a round million folk must be in London. Those great bare heights, with a purity of sky above and behind them, are always there, waiting for you.'
>
> ***English Journey*** (1984)

His happy home life was broken only by quarrels with his father about Sundays in Bradford. Jonathan Priestley was an intolerant Sabbatarian, who denounced any attempt to bring colour and gaiety into the drab tedium of an English provincial Sunday. For the young Priestley, his father's 'chapel' Sundays were abhorrent.

> 'He had the kind of Sunday night he liked while I, wanting the theatre and music, and encounters with pretty girls in cafes was debarred from my kind of Sunday evening...'
>
> ***The Listener***, July 1959.

Culturally, Bradford offered the young writer all that he needed. It was a vibrant and progressive city in the forefront of social change. Bradford set its own civilised pace, it did not need to look elsewhere for such standards; certainly not to London, which played little or no part in Jonathan Priestley's life.

> 'which was entirely based on the north; he rarely read London newspapers; and he cared no more about London than it did about him. He was very much a West Riding man'.
>
> ***The Listener***, July 1959.

Edwardian Bradford possessed a unique cultural scene with a quality all of its own. There was a cultural optimism about the town similar to that of Liverpool in the 1960s. Priestley sought to recapture this quality in several of his literary works. For all its provincialism Bradford was international in its outlook, the wool trade had seen to that.

> 'And then there was this curious leaven of intelligent aliens, chiefly German-Jews and mostly affluent... that small colony of foreign or mixed Bradfordians produced some men of great distinction, including a famous composer, two renowned painters and a well known poet. There was then this odd mixture in pre-war Bradford. A dash of the Rhine and the Oder found its way into our grim runnel t' mucky beck.

Bradford was determinedly Yorkshire and provincial, yet some of its suburbs reached as far as Frankfurt or Leipzig.'

English Journey (1984)

Bradford's German colony had been settled in the town as wool merchants since the 1840s and they brought a rich cultural catalyst to Bradford's solid West Riding scene. But the First World War soon changed that as the German merchanting houses altered their names or went out of business altogether. The war changed Priestley's life too, for in August 1914

'when the newsboys were running and shouting everyday and all day. I was alone in the house, my family being at the seaside. I waited until they came back before I enlisted in early September.'

A year later he left for France with the 10th Duke of Wellington's regiment, never to return as a permanent Bradfordian. He was buried alive by a trench mortar, gassed during an attack on the Western front in the summer of 1918 but survived the holocaust unlike many of his Bradford friends. Priestley's Bradford ended in 1914. He returned only as a visitor but no one thinks of him without thinking of Bradford. That progressive, pioneering, reforming city shaped his formative years, and influenced much of his later writing, existing as a real economic and cultural world and yet offering him a spiritual vision for which to live, and create, a lost world,

'Bradford, where I was born and where I lived the most exciting and perhaps the most important years of my life. To me, Bradford is not one manufacturing town out of many, a place to be visited and sketched; it is not really a town at all, it is a vast series of pictures in time and space; it is an autobiographical library; it is a hundred thousand succeeding states of mind, it is my childhood and youth; it is a lost world.'

And so it was, for Priestley's early life had coincided with the nadir of Bradford's golden age as a classic nineteenth century provincial city. It was a unique experience in urban history and to one of its favourite sons, a special place, indeed.

'The Bradford of those years was no ordinary city... In those pre-1914 days Bradford was considered the most progressive place in the United Kingdom... I am prepared to bet that Bradford produced more well known people – musicians, scientists, writers, performers and the like than any place anything like its size in the whole kingdom...'

Preface to *Socialism Over 60 Years* (1946)

From this brief introduction to a Bradford that is gone, turn now to the photographs and written words of two men who sought to encapsulate the essence of Bradford when it was a very vibrant and progressive English provincial city.

Gary Firth

Plate camera and accessories used by the young Christopher Pratt to take many of the photographs in this book.

Bygone Bradford

Much of the centre of Bradford is located in a 'basin like feature' enclosed by high lands all around, except for the valley of the North Brook leading to the River Aire (Canal Road). This amphitheatre of the local landscape posed serious environmental problems when the steam age arrived. From hundreds of chimneys a sulphurous pall of smoke hovered over the centre of the town, blotting out much of the natural light. This murky roof-top view overlooks the warehousing area of 'Little Germany'; from here the city's merchant princes controlled an important export industry.

'Lost in its smokey valley among the Pennine hills, bristling with tall mill chimneys with its face of blackened stone Bruddersford is generally held to be an ugly city: and so, I suppose it is: but it always seemed to me to have the kind of ugliness that could not only be tolerated but often enjoyed; it was grim but not mean.'

Bright Day *(1946)*

For many Bradford children 'laikin' aht' meant going through the ritual of some game or song at a favourite, and often sacred, location on the street. The high priest or priestess, usually the oldest child, chose the game order, excluded certain unwanted parties and reminded those who remained of the rules. Here in a court off the bottom of Leeds Road, the photographer beautifully captures this ritual. Perhaps the young lady is introducing 'On a mountain lived a lady' or 'A big ship sailed' or 'There came three dukes a riding'?

'I had been brought up in a West Riding industrial community, where to a youngster the social hierarchy was invisible. I am not pretending we had a miniature classless society there, but we probably came nearer to having one than anybody born in southern England can ever imagine.'

Margin Released (1962)

Toller lane as young Priestley knew it. Here the open topped tram is making its way into the leafy suburb of Manningham on the Duckworth Lane – Sunbridge Road route. In the second photograph Bradford secondary school pupils are poised for some 'systematic hard slogging'.

'More than half a century ago, living then in Toller Lane, Bradford, but all in another world, I was sixteen and I had to make a choice. I had to leave that summer or I had to stay there to work for a university scholarship. No compromise was possible. There was not a chance of hanging on at school for a year or two, not doing very much. Neither the school nor my father, who had once taught there, would have tolerated it. You stayed on to begin some systematic hard slogging for scholarship. Contrary to some reports, I have never been at any age a systematic hard slogger.'

Members of the Southend Hall Boys Brigade gymnastics club sometime in 1908.

'Games I enjoyed, and even collected three medals, which vanished years ago. (But where do such indestructible things go?) Gymnastics I detested then and have never admired since; those Czech mass antics seem to me a horror, halfway to the anthill. Most of the hours spent in classrooms were tedious.'

Margin Released (1962)

Christopher Pratt captures the fun and jollity of a Methodist Sunday school sports day before the First War.

The sports and games—sing, heavenly muse! would ask for epic treatment. I should begin with our daily scuffles in the dark sheds with little indiarubber balls, and end with our triumphs, a-glitter with cups and shields, on the field of tug-of-war and football.

Essays of Reminiscence,
to celebrate Belle Vue School Jubilee, 1927

The woodwork class of Green Lane Board School in 1901 where Priestley's father was teacher and which the young Priestley often passed on his way to Belle Vue School.

'It is equally useless my attempting to describe my adventures with woodwork and ironwork, in what was to me that hateful place across the school yard. How I loathed that sawing and chiselling and filing.'

Essays of Reminiscence (1927)

Opposite: Young men find pleasure in a game of 'marbles', 'taws', or glass 'alleys' at the junction of George Street and Brooklyn Street with the recently built (1902) Eastbrook Hall in the background. In the second photograph older boys and young men gather at a Bradford street corner in 1904 to insult the girls and scorn the respectful. The members of such a gang had usually left school, worked part-time by running errands for building labourers, mill workmen and foundrymen. The 'gang' had its own unwritten constitution and membership rules and stalked a certain territory, trespass on which provoked street-gang wars.

'Children made their own fun instead of having it concocted for them by film and radio. Perhaps it is against my own interest, as one of those experts to declare that they are better off than the passive mobs of filmgoers and radio listeners of today but I feel strongly that they were.'

*Article in **Telegraph & Argus**, June 1946*

Bradford Park Avenue had been officially admitted into the Second Division of the Football League in the 1908-9 season having been formed in 1907 and played in the Southern League in their first season. This was the squad of players with which they began their Football League history in August 1908. They played at the former rugby ground in Horton Park Avenue and here they can be seen in front of the bowling green pavilion. Under the management of George Gillies (seated far left second row) and captaincy of G. T. Craig, they consolidated their position in the league. Seated in the centre is goalkeeper Tom Baddeley who had played for Wolves and England before coming to Bradford. Priestley's trial was as a full back but he obviously failed to impress the Park Avenue staff.

'I played a great deal of soccer and at the age of sixteen appeared in the trials at Bradford Park Avenue.'

Yorkshire Observer, *November 1947*

Wool clerks, hard at work at the Bradford Wool Conditioning House after the First War.

'I left school to become a very junior clerk with Helm and Company, Swan Arcade, Bradford. I was not the office boy. Low as I was, there was one even lower. At times, however, we were between office boys, and then I had to fill ink-wells, put out blotting paper, uncover the typewriters, work the copying press, and take enormous bundles of samples to the General Post office, a chore I particularly detested.'

Margin Released *(1962)*

Swan Arcade, shortly before its demolition in 1964, showing Priestley's Market Street entrance.

'Swan Arcade, where we had our office, several floors up, had entrances in three different streets—and very high imposing entrances they were too—but the main approach, which happened to be the one nearest to my tram, was from Market Street. I thought it a fine street during those years, and now, looking back, I do not believe youth and inexperience were deceiving me. Unlike the other streets in the centre of the town, it was not too narrow and it was level. Unlike them too, it had a metropolitan look, an air of massive opulence; it was a thoroughfare fit for men who would, as they said, 'cut up for a pretty penny'. Now that it has been tastelessly improved, it has lost all character; but in those days its solid buildings of smoke-blackened stone, unbroken by facades that looked bright for a month and then a dingy mistake ever afterwards, pleased the eye.'

Margin Released (1962)

'This does not mean I disliked Swan Arcade itself. To begin with, I am an arcade man, and suspect that only some unsleeping evil principle, for ever at work among us English, prevents our having more of them. Moreover, Swan Arcade was no ordinary roofed-over huddle of gift shops; it was on the grand scale. (I prefer the past tense because even now machines, secretly directed by that evil principle, may be clawing it down to spread the glass-and-concrete monotony from Brasilia to Bradford.) When it was opened in 1879, it was saluted as 'the most complete building of its kind in Yorkshire, if not in England.' But this description, doing it the barest justice, does not deserve to be called a salute . . .

Among English arcades it was a giant, five storeys high. The skylights were so far above my head that I hardly ever gave then a glance. I seem to remember up there an airy clutter and complication of galleries, windows, straight and curved metal supports and struts. At each corner were stairs and lifts going up to various office floors, premises like ours; between these corners, inside the building, were smaller blocks of offices and what the trade called the 'market rooms'; and along the ground-floor aisled, beneath the forgotten skylights, which were of a sort to keep the interior darkish, were no ordinary shops (the original and highly sensible intention was to have them there, and of course there was opposition) but rather gloomy agencies and establishments, the kind that had brown wire screens in the windows to dishearten common people.'

Margin Released (1962)

The photograph above and Priestley's words say it all. Priestley was strongly opposed to the demolition of Swan Arcade and never quite forgave Bradford for this act of self-mutilation.

By 1911, when Priestley became a junior clerk in the wool sorting firm of Helm & Co, the Bradford worsted trade was already moving down the production cycle by supplying foreign countries with combed tops as they developed their own weaving and spinning processes. Here, the raw wool arrives at the Conditioning House in Cape Street, off Canal road.

'Our firm exported tops—wool that had been washed and combed and was ready to be spun into yarn—to spinners and manufacturers on the Continent. It bought raw wool, mostly at summer sales held in places like Andover, Marlborough, Devizes, sorted and blended it according to one formula or another, then sent it to the combing mills; and after much posting of samples to places all over Europe, and even as far as Rhode Island, we took such orders as came for these various tops of ours.'

Margin Released *(1962)*

The wool office at the Conditioning House. By 1912 the home grown wool supply was diminishing in comparison to the growing imports of colonial wool from Australia and New Zealand, particularly as a result of cross breeding merino flocks with long-woolled Lincolns.

'...I used to think that a wool office—and I was sent to one for a season—was the very symbol of the prosaic; but now I see that I was wrong. Revisiting them again, I saw that these offices, with their bins of samples, blue-wrapped cylinders of hair, are really romantic. Take down some of those greasy or dusty samples and you bring the ends of the earth together. This wool was lately wandering about on our own South Downs. This comes from the Argentine, this from Australia. The dust and dried dung that falls out of this packet comes from the desert. Here, in this blue paper, is hair clipped from the belly of a camel. These wools and hairs will be sorted, scoured, combed, the long strands forming Tops, the short Noils, and these Tops and Noils, if they are not used locally, may be exported all over the place, from Finland to Spain. What they will end as, God only knows. Their adventures are terrific.'

English Journey (1984)

Refrigerated shipping in the 1880s enabled the import of foreign lamb and mutton, further encouraging the Australasian sheep farmers in rearing cross breds. Colonial wool growers sent their fleeces to brokers in England for sale at the London Colonial Wool Auction or at the Bradford Wool Exchange in Market Street, the rear of which can be seen centre left of this photograph.

PARKER (the business man now): *I see Crossbreds are down again.*

HELLIWELL (another business man): *Ay—and they'll stay down with Australian market as it is. If I've said it once, I've said it a thousand times—if Merinos is down and staying down, then your Crossbreds'll have to follow. Now, look at Merinos——*

MARIA (looking up to expostulate): *Here, Joe, we didn't come here to talk about Merinos. This isn't Wool Exchange.'*

When We Are Married (1938)

O.

In 1901 57,000 Bradfordians were employed in textile manufacture. The majority of women worked in the spinning and weaving departments of the city's mills. Sorting, combing and dyeing chiefly employed men. Before 1914, Bradford is thought to have handled, in some way or other, five-sixths of the wool in this country. Every wool transaction, from exporting the raw material to retailing the finished piece, was dealt with in Bradford. In 1910 the city's annual turnover in textiles was estimated at ninety million pounds.

'I much preferred the atmosphere of the firm's warehouse, where the wool arrived to be sorted. This was about half a mile away, not too close to Market Street and the centre of the city, on the near edge of a whole region of warehouses and mills.'

Margin Released (1962)

The Bradford Conditioning House in Canal Road. The first premises were at the rear of the Town Hall but in 1902 were transferred here. In 1891 the Chamber of Commerce had suggested some kind of testing centre for checking the moisture content and other properties of raw wool. Priestley would have made numerous visits to this building with wool samples from the warehouse of Helm & Company.

'Thus whenever I was sent to the warehouse which was about ten minutes' walk away or along to the Conditioning House, only another ten minutes' walk, I took three or four times as long as I ought to have done. One reason for this was that I had already started to smoke a pipe and unlike most wool offices, no smoking was allowed in ours.'

The Clerk, *April 1966*

In 1893, standing outside the Labour Institute, a former chapel in Peckover Street, are the men and one woman, Katherine St. John Conway, who founded the Independent Labour Party following an inaugural conference at the Institute. In attendance was George Bernard Shaw, Keir Hardie, Robert Blatchford and Ben Tillett. The Manningham ward soon elected Tillett to the Bradford council, as one of this country's earliest socialist councillors.

'A few were rich, and a great many were very poor, working from morning until night for miserable wages; but they were all one lot of folk, and Jack not only thought himself as good as his master but very often told him so. Bradford was not only provincial but also fiercely democratic. (The Independent Labour Party was born there.)'

English Journey *(1984)*

J. B. Priestley, unlike his father, was never a member of the Labour Party although he was entirely sympathetic to its ideals of social justice and the removal of poverty. In 1946 he wrote a preface to Fenner Brockway's biography of Fred Jowett, a Bradfordian whose name is inseparable from the early British Socialist movement. In it, Priestley did not hesitate to compare modern socialism with that of the pre-1914 Labour movement which had 'an enthusiasm and breadth of appeal largely missing from the modern Labour Party'.

'I grew up in this English socialist tradition, and at heart I still believe in it. Liberalism is modern man's nearest approach to real civilisation; as soon as most of it was sneered away, the power men took over, the secret police arrived, torture came back. This old-fashioned English left was liberalism with the starch out of it, the fire lit, the company it could assemble more varied, easier and warmer-hearted, not incapable of a song and a chorus. It was life-seeking, life-enhancing.'

Margin Released *(1962)*

F. PALEY

It must be distinctly understood that "Round the Hearth" is pre-eminently a personal feature, so that the opinions expressed therein are not necessarily those of the paper itself. Letters dealing with subjects treated in "Round the Hearth" are invited, and should be addressed to "J. B. P. c/o BRADFORD PIONEER."—ED.

Children's Competition.

After carefully reading through the many essays I have received in connection with the above competition. I you can make yourselves? Often when reading a poem happy thoughts seem to flit everywhere, all your dull thoughts seem to disappear. Often that same

Keep your eyes open for another co petition and better luck next time.

The Bradford Playgoers' Society.

This Society held its first ann meeting in Channing Hall a short ti ago. The room at the Arts Club l lately proved to be too small for meetings and readings and the co mittee has decided to use Chann Hall next winter. The first open-reading took place some weeks ago the grounds of the Myddleton Ho Ilkley, and the experiment was an qualified success, partly due, probal to the play chosen—"Prunella," t delightful fantasy by Lawrence Ho man, and Granville Barker. Mr. Lishman has been elected chairman the Society for the next season, and

There was quite a distinct cultural aspect to socialist life in pre-1914 Bradford; it included socialist Sunday schools, a Labour cricket league and a whole range of club activities including, singing, cycling, dancing and walking clubs. Jowett himself had formed the Bradford Labour Church as early as 1891. There were socialist newspapers and journals circulating the town and J. B. Priestley wrote a weekly review of the Bradford cultural scene in the Labour journal the 'Bradford Pioneer', under the editorship of Alfred Pickles. His 'Round the Hearth' feature gained him free access to local theatres and music halls.

'What happened was that from January to October, 1913, I wrote a column entitled 'Round The Hearth' for a little Labour weekly, the 'Bradford Pioneer'. This was of course journalism of the humblest sort, and unpaid at that. Nobody made a penny out of this pioneering. Mine was the cultural department, filled with paragraphs about books, concerts and plays; the rest of the paper, I feel certain though I cannot recall any of it, was narrowly and fiercely political. Bradford, the birthplace of the Independent Labour Party, was one of the earliest socialists strongholds. My father and many, though not all, of his friends were socialists. They were not Marxists – and I doubt if there was a student of economics among them – but were all in the looser and warmer English tradition of socialism.'

Margin Released *(1962)*

The Lyons Tea & Coffee House, according to a Bradford directory for 1912, was at 57, Market Street, i.e. at the Town Hall end adjoining the King's Arcade and John Shelton & Sons, hosiers. The gentleman on the extreme right of this photograph is just leaving the cafe.

'The cafe where we spent so much time and so little money was a Lyons in Market Street. It was a long narrow place divided by a short flight of stairs. The solid customers munched away on the ground level; we golden lads, without even a glance around made straight for the upper level, the back room you might say, where we were capable of monopolising a couple of tables for hours while spending about sixpence a head.'

Margin Released *(1962)*

Young men relax in a Bradford club.

'I was already acquainted with several young reporters, whose sophistication seemed to me almost satanic; they could take the city to pieces over a coffee and roll-and-butter at Lyons's; they had even interviewed delectable beings appearing at the Theatre Royal or the Empire; they were already men of the world to my stammering oaf.'

Margin Released *(1962)*

About to reach its terminus at the bottom of Sunbridge Road, this tram, a double decker, had been brought into commission by the council in 1903. It had a seating capacity of 51 but was restructured in the years immediately following the First World War.

'I still lived at home, though in a more detached fashion, in Saltburn Place, Toller Lane. I still took the tram from Duckworth Lane to its terminus at the bottom of Sunbridge Road, and then walked along Market Street to Swan Arcade, pretending to be a junior clerk in a wool office.'

Margin Released (1962)

The children of Green Lane ready to tuck into the school meal provided by the ratepayers of Bradford. There had been a tradition of subsidised feeding of needy children in Bradford since 1892. When the Bradford School Board was replaced by the Bradford Education Committee in 1902 it immediately sought permission from the Board of Education in London to provide meals for poor children out of public funding. After several experiments, some privately financed, the Committee eventually in 1907 built a central cooking depot alongside Jonathan Priestley's school at Green Lane. Here, headmaster Priestley is flanked by two older girls of the school.

'My father was a schoolmaster, and a very good one, with an almost ludicrous passion for acquiring and imparting knowledge. He was not a born scholar, but he was a born teacher. Outside his school, he did a great deal of useful public service—speaking, helping to organise, working on committees, and so on—not because he was a busybody or was socially ambitious, but because he was essentially public-spirited, the type of citizen that democratic theorists have in mind but rarely in actual view. But there was nothing of the smooth committee humbug about him. He was very brisk, humorous, stout-hearted, not to be patronised or bullied.'

Midnight on the Desert (1937)

Priestley supervises the weighing of the children in his care for the guidance of Bradford's Medical Officer of Health.

'Now my father, who knew Jowett well, was the headmaster of a large elementary school in Bradford. It was situated in a poorish neighbourhood though called, with some irony, Green Lane School. And it was at my father's school that the first children in this country received school meals and we knew all about it at home because this piece of social service, considered a revolutionary step then, attracted a good deal of attention in both the local and national press with the further result that photographs of my father weighing some children were widely published.'

Preface to **Socialism Over Sixty Years** (1946)

Bradford's Edwardian poor helped each other. Families, little better off than each other, came to the help of neighbours when times were hard, although living as close to each other as these people did, did not always lead to friendship and to the cosy community spirit that some writers, including Priestley, would have us believe. Here 'a cup of sugar' or 'a mashing of tea' has been borrowed from some kindly neighbour.

'... it was easy for neighbours to become friends, and people never dreamt of living that boxed-up lonely life which left so many suburban housewives on edge during the Nineteen Thirties. Modest and informal hospitality was easy then and was taken for granted. Hence the popping in.'

Bright Day (1946), p.22

Pratt's photograph captures the street life of a Bradford off licence at the turn of the century. Ale was often bought by the jug from the 'outdoor department', particularly by families where the wife insisted on her share of pleasure and drank at home. Men who did not drink were regarded as 'henpecked' or 'miseries' and were certainly something less than normal.

'His own family were mill workers, both men and women, but a solid steady sort; but he had plucked my mother, my real mother, about whom I knew nothing except that she was high-spirited and witty, from the clogs and shawls 'back o't mill', a free and easy, rather raffish kind of working-class life, where in the grim little back-to-back houses they shouted and screamed, laughed and cried, and sent out a jug for more beer.'

Margin Released (1962)

Bradford had long been a centre of dissent. Methodism had been established there since 1744 but by 1900 the majority of Bradfordians did not attend church, easing their conscience by making their children go to Sunday school. Here the Eastbrook Methodist Brotherhood do their Wesleyan Missionary work at the bottom of Birk Street in 1907, bringing a brief burst of glory with their gospel singing and salvation bands. However, working people remained unimpressed and continued to ignore the authority of the religious establishment.

'I heard music and discovered that a Salvation Army band was playing just round the corner; it was playing quite well too; and a considerable crowd had collected. So far as I could judge only the innermost ring of this crowd was in search of salvation; the others were listening idly to the music, smoking their pipes, and waiting until the pubs opened.'

English Journey *(1984)*

Mr. Popplewell's 'outdoor department' once again. This time one of the lower class of women who had been brave enough to enter licenced premises beats a hasty beshawled retreat with a jug of beer (?) secreted under her apron. On the right a group of happy mill girls whose smiles suggest the end of a working day.

'It is true that the women and girls who worked in the mills then were no models for feminine refinement. Sometimes, when I finished earlier than usual at the office and walked home, the route I preferred took me past one of the largest mills in the district, often just when the women were coming out. I would find myself breasting a tide of shawls, and something about my innocent dandyism would set them screaming at me, and what I heard then, though I was never a prudish lad, made my cheeks burn. And it was still the custom, in some mills if not in that particular one, for the women to seize a newly-arrived lad and 'sun' him, that is, pull his trousers down and reveal his genitals. But all this is not unwholesome and perhaps traditional female bawdiness—there was a suggestion of mythology, ancient worship, folklore, about that queer 'sunning' ritual— was far removed from cynical whoring. There was nothing sly, nothing hypocritical, about these coarse dames and screaming lasses, who were devoted to their own men, generally working in the same mill, and kept on 'courting', though the actual courtship stage was over early, for years and years until a baby was due . . .'

Margin Released *(1962)*

52

Two mill girl sisters pose like professional models for Christopher Pratt in 1908. Their brief childhood is at an end as they hover on the threshold of womanhood, innocently unshawled; for a working class woman, even if she slipped next door, would do so with a shawl on. To be seen in public without a shawl provoked street gossip-mongers and accusations of 'indecency'.

'No doubt the young males were often merely predatory—though the worst of them never paraded the park, but, like two older men I knew slightly, lurked elsewhere, bent on seducing half-witted housemaids— but the girls, wearing their best clothes and usually in arm-linked trios and quartets, must have known very well, in spite of their glad-eyeing, whispering and giggling, that it was here, not in the mill or office, not even at home or at the chapel bazaar, that they were engaged in the serious business of life.'

Such Edwardian beauties as Miss Gabrielle Ray brought glamour, beauty and not a little fantasy to the drab monotonous lives of Bradford's working population. Here Miss Ray can be seen in the part of Maid Marian in Frances Laidler's 'Babes in the Wood' pantomime at the Prince's Theatre in 1919.

'Actresses, wickedly painted even off the stage, were even more remote, hardly related biographically to the women and girls one knew, belonging to other orders of being, fays and sylphs.'

Margin Released (1962)

Lovely ladies like Miss Ray were not typical of Edwardian womanhood. The woman on the common Bradford scene was old before her time, wrinkle featured, a mouthful of blackened stubs and a back bent with childbearing and endless hours spent on domestic cleaning. Here, an elderly woman acts as street 'knocker-up' dressed in the standard clothing for all Bradford working-class women, clogs and shawl.

'but his mother, never downcast, always blazing-eyed, about six-and-a-half stone of indomitable femininity, was the greater character. Even several months after George had left for Cambridge, after I had dutifully admired all the things he had to take with him, the flannels, the dinner jacket, and the rest, I caught sight of her one very cold morning on my way to work. She was coming out of an office building, for once looking shrunken and fagged, after the cleaning she must have taken on to help pay for all those things so necessary for Cambridge.'

Margin Released (1962)

Despite the constant pall of smoke hovering over the city and the squalor of high density living, most people tried to keep themselves and their possessions clean. Some housewives gave their lives to polishing furniture, black-leading fire irons and washing clothes in the peggy tub. One or two became obsessed by it, the front room was always the Sunday room when dust sheets, even newspapers, were removed. This photograph shows the 'technology' of a working class washday, mangle, peggy tub, posser and, out of sight, a large bar of carbolic soap.

'When days really were days and each had a character of its own, when I was a boy up Toller Lane, Bradford, there was no mistaking Monday. You could smell it just as you could smell Thursday which was baking day in our house. Monday, of course, was washing day. It was a day when the house was fairly lost in soap suds and steam. It was a day when mothers and wives and sisters were very busy and apt to be short tempered. Menfolk were only there on sufferance, and if they had any sense and didn't want to be reminded of their various weaknesses by irate females, they crept about the house, carefully avoiding the baskets of wet clothes and the rickety clothes horses near every fire.'

Home Service broadcast, *June 1943*

Market Street, seen from the junction with Booth Street (left) and Lower Cheapside (right). In the distance, through the smog, is Town Hall Square and the Wool Exchange.

'To go along Canal Road on a warm day, as I often had to do, passing between a sulphuric acid works and a hide-and-skin establishment (is there a worse reek?) was to know an olfactory ordeal. But there was a centre-of-Bradford smell, there in Market Street, except when the rains were washing it away, characteristic and unmistakable, and not acrid, not unpleasant, though there was smoke and a touch of soot in it that my nose is glad to remember.'

Margin Released (1962)

Town Hall Square, c 1910, with a busy Market Street in the background. This is the terminus for the tram service to Queensbury. The crowd of people on the right is awaiting a tram in specially constructed, moveable stations. Steam trams had first been introduced to Bradford in 1882 but were superseded by electric traction after 1898. The building in the centre of the photograph is the Refreshment House of the Bradford Coffee Tavern Company.

'...the great double-decked electric tram, already often mentioned but never celebrated had gone groaning and stopping and starting again, "the high-built glittering galleon of the streets"; maddening of course yet more than indisposable, a kind of clumsy comrade, hardly our horse, perhaps our immense camel, our illuminated elephant. It took us to and from work, drama and music, encounters with girls; it could turn our faces to the moors, untarnished heights and clean air.'

Margin Released (1962)

Kirkgate Market, better known as 't' Spice Market', was built in 1871 as a shopping arcade close to the site of the old Manor Hall and on the site of a former market. This handsome shopping centre with its friendly little stalls was beloved of many Bradfordians. Many will remember the lavish portico of the Kirkgate entrance with its symbols of flowers and fruit and a seemingly endless flight of stone steps to the point shown in this photograph. In the corner, a favourite toy shop of the author's, where grandma bought many a toy soldier or Dinky car.

'Among the latter was the covered Market, our nearest approach to the Oriental bazaar. The stalls there are not temporary affairs but permanent fixtures, shops without windows, and most of them have been in the same hands ever since I can remember. On one side there are still queer old-fashioned little eating places, where you tuck into boiled cod and steak pie sitting in pews. On the other side are the music stalls, where if you linger a second the assistants pounce upon you at once and conjure the florins out of your pocket. It was at one of these stalls, years ago when I was a schoolboy, that I bought, in a lunatic fit, that most melancholy instrument, a one-stringed fiddle. It cost a pound or two, and I paid for it, laboriously, in shillings and sixpences. 'You oughtn't to do that,' observed the assistant, a supercilious young man. 'Looks as if you've been saving up.' And as that was precisely what I had been doing, I was lost in shame. (A month or two afterwards, I swopped that one-stringed fiddle for a deer-stalker hat, owned by a friend of mine, who had about as much use for it as he would have for the fiddle, or as I really had for either.) Between the music at one extreme and the boiled cod in pews at the other, there are rows and rows of drapery, boot and shoe, confectionery, grocery stalls.'

English Journey (1984)

The German community first settled in Bradford in the 1830s and 1840s when German textile merchants shifted their places of business from Leeds to Bradford. Eventually they established a distinct commercial zone with the impressive warehouses of Little Germany but they also raised the cultural tone of Victorian Bradford through art, literature and music. The continuing tradition of the Halle concerts is attributed largely to Bradford's German community. By the 1890s, international events fostered a clear anti-German feeling in Britain and on the outbreak of the First World War Bradford's German families changed their names and opted for anonymity. Although these Germans were of the Jewish faith the majority tended to be adherents of the Jewish Reform movement. They drew little strength from their Judaism and were more in tune with the Christianity of Unitarianism. This vestige of the German connection with Bradford shows the Deutsche Evangelische Kirche in Great Horton Road.

'And then there was this curious leaven of intelligent aliens, chiefly German-Jews and mostly affluent. They were so much a part of the place when I was a boy that it never occurred to me to ask why they were there. I saw their outlandish names on office doors, knew that they lived in certain pleasant suburbs, and obscurely felt that they had always been with us and would always remain. That small colony of foreign or mixed Bradfordians some men of great distinction, including a famous composer, two renowned painters, and a well-known poet. (In Humbert Woolfe's 'Now a Stranger' you get a glimpse of what life was like in that colony for at least one small boy.) I can remember when one of the best-known clubs in Bradford was Schillerverein, and in those days a Londoner was a stranger sight than a German. There was, then, this odd mixture in pre-war Bradford. A dash of the Rhine and the Oder found its way into our grim runnel – 't' mucky beck.' Bradford was determinedly Yorkshire and provincial, yet some of its suburbs reached as far as Frankfort and Leipzig. It was odd enough. But it worked.*

English Journey (1984)

The 'civic pride' of Bradford's Victorian councillors led to the erection of the Town Hall in 1873. This front elevation in local sandstone houses statues of the kings and queens of England. The elegant Italianate tower of 200 feet makes an impressive landmark to the city skyline. As a boy, Priestley would have seen the extension of the Town Hall, a part of which can be seen to the left in the second photograph.

'Part of me is still in Bradford, and can never leave it, though when I return there now I wander about half-lost, a melancholy stranger. I am in the right place but not at the right time. But in the world outside, as I move from Stockholm to Montreal, Tokio to Santiago, Chile, something at the core of me is still in Market Street hearing the Town Hall chimes.'

Margin Released *(1962)*

There was very little open space in the heavily built up centre of Bradford which had serious consequences for the health and recreational opportunities of the common people. Bradford's public parks and cemeteries became havens of quiet and fresh air. The first public park, Peel Park, was opened in 1863. Seven years later the textile magnate Samuel Lister offered his Manningham deer park to the corporation for £40,000 and Lister Park was the result.

'My father and his friends were always among the thousands in the tiers of chairs that curved round the bandstand, though not entirely enclosing it. They were concert-going as well as sitting in the open, smoking their pipes; they could be critical, and were not to be brassed and cymballed into appreciation; and I have listened more than once to a close friend of my father's – a happy man who had a tiny business he could leave any time for expeditions and cricket matches, company and the discussion of fine points – explaining why the clarinets of the Scots Guards, his favourites, were superior to those of the Irish or the Coldstream. High above the nearest row of chairs, higher than the top of the bandstand itself, was a promenade, and there the youth of our part of Bradford— Lister Park not being far from where I lived—congregated densely, some of the lads and girls packed along the rails.'

Margin Released *(1962)*

Another scheme to occupy the recreational time of the working classes and deflect them from drink and drunkenness was St. George's Hall, largely the work of Samuel Smith, an early Bradford mayor, with a successful dyeing business in the town. Smith's part in the inquiry into the Moral Condition of Bradford in 1849 had convinced him of the need to find alternative music to that of Bradford's several hundred beer shops and public houses. Smith's idea for a public concert hall was strongly backed by German merchants like Steinthal, Sichel, Behrens and Waud. Built to a Lockwood and Mawson design (like the Town Hall and Wool Exchange) this magnificent building attracted Rubinstein, von Bulow and Charles Halle after it opened in 1853.

'When I was in my teens, and would sit in the shilling gallery, peering down at old Richter taking the Halle Orchestra through Beethoven, Brahms and Wagner, or occasionally staring entranced at the pale dynamic Nikisch handling the London Symphony Orchestra, I would come reeling down that long stone flight of stairs, drunk with music, my head starrier than the night.'

Midnight on the Desert (1937)

'Gladstone Hall was nothing to look at—it was a square ugly building seating about four thousand people—but it made a fine concert hall, and its acoustics, especially in the great gallery, were magnificent. My ticket, which worked out at ninepence a concert, was for one of the Side Galleries, the North Gallery.'

Bright Day (1946)

Two Bradford theatres. Firstly, the Theatre Royal in Manningham Lane, which had opened at Christmas as early as 1864. Under the management of Charles Rice, comedian and playwright, the theatre flourished. Particularly successful were Rice's pantomimes. In the second photograph is another old Bradford theatre, the Prince's, which opened in 1875 under the management of William Morgan. Two years later it was gutted by fire; it had a precarious existence until 1886 when it was taken over by Henry Pullan and Francis Laidler, Bradford's 'King of Pantomime'. It provided 'live' theatre until 1964 and Bradfordians will remember it as a fine repertory theatre which premiered several of J. B. Priestley's early plays. Underneath the Prince's were the premises of the People's Palace, formerly the Star Music Hall, whose comedians, illusionists and traditional music hall acts were so attractive to Priestley and others until its closure in May 1938.

'I had reservations about a certain type of gentlemanly melodrama then in vogue: I remember one called A White Man appearing at the Theatre Royal, between Benson's Shakespeare and Edward Compton's Sheridan and Goldsmith, these pieces seemed contrived and anaemic, inferior to the full-blooded melodrama we had every week at the other theatre, the Prince's—A Royal Divorce, The Face at the Window, and the like. Yes, in my teens I could be said to be stagestruck, and it was an advantage to me long afterward, when I came to work in the theatre, that I had left this complaint far behind, like the measles and mumps of my childhood.'

Margin Released (1962)

1. The Syncophonics
2. George Robey
3. Little Tich
4. Miss Vesta Tilley

'And sometimes in company with my Uncle Miles, given a night off by Aunt Hilda, I would go to the second "house" of the Imperial Music Hall, where in our worn plush seats in the dress-circle, price one-and-sixpence, we would listen to Little Tich and George Robey, Vesta Tilley and Maidie Scott (a deliciously saucy comedienne), Jack and Evelyne (and he was a superb improvising droll), and a glorious comic with a round face and an impossible moustache and an indescribably ridiculous manner, one of the best comics I ever saw, who drank hard and died young, called Jimmy Learmouth.'

Bright Day (1946)

'And once we had Little Tich, released from the Tivoli, to dazzle the suburbs. Uncle Nick, who had appeared with him abroad, knew him well, and I was introduced to him, a solemn little Mr. Relph, who talked to me about painting. On the stage he might be a barrister in court, a tipsy man-about-town, a regal lady encumbered with an enormous train, but always he set these miniature beings blazing with a mad energy, as if, coming from a different species, they were flaming burlesques of our own larger dim idiocies. And just once we had Grock, who hadn't been long in England then and hadn't reached the height of his fame, but even then was the best clown I ever saw except Chaplin. He was like a serious, humble but hopeful visitor from another planet, endlessly defeated by alien and hostile circumstances, and like Chaplin he brought your laughter close to the beginning of tears.'

Lost Empires (1965)

'One evening there, hot and astonished in the Empire, we discovered ragtime, brought to us by three young Americans: Hedges Brothers and Jacobsen, they called themselves. It was as if we had been still living in the nineteenth century and then suddenly found the twentieth glaring and screaming at us. We were yanked into our own age, fascinating, jungle-haunted, monstrous. We were used to being sung at in music-halls in a robust and zestful fashion, but the syncopated frenzy of these three young Americans was something quite different; shining with sweat, they almost hung over the footlights, defying us to resist the rhythm, gradually hypnotising us chanting and drumming us into another kind of life in which anything might happen. All right, what we were hearing for the first time was Alexander's Ragtime Band, Waiting for the Robert E. Lee.'

Margin Released (1962)

The Empire Theatre, fronted by the Alexandra Hotel, was opened in January 1899 as a once nightly variety theatre as opposed to the two legitimate theatres, the Royal and the Prince's. Here, knockabout comedians, female impersonators and pretty ballad singers trod the boards until the pressure from the nearby Alhambra Theatre (1914) and a serious fire enforced its closure. It was reopened after the First War and from here the British National Opera Company was begun in February 1922. The billboard in this photograph advertises 'The Woman in White'.

'Bradford then had two theatres and two music halls, all under our patronage. I was especially fond of the fourpenny balcony at the Empire— not the cheapest seats for there was a twopenny gallery behind us— where I forgot my discomfort—the expert 'packers' treated us like sardines.'

Margin Released *(1962)*

Bradford's first municipal library had been opened in Tyrrel Street in 1872 but six years later was transferred to new premises in the recently opened Kirkgate Market precinct where it remained until 1966. The reading rooms were situated half way up the left hand side of this pre-first war view of Darley Street.

'We were playing three consecutive weeks in the West Riding—first Bradford, then Leeds, then Sheffield, which meant we should have no long Sunday train journeys. And I knew Bradford pretty well, having been fairly often, and I knew that if the weather was no good for outdoor sketching—and now, with no more rehearsing, I was free all day—I could go to the Cartwright Memorial Hall or to the Reference Library in Darley Street to look through some special numbers of 'The Studio'.'

Lost Empires (1965)

Walking or rambling had become a popular pastime by 1914 and most northern industrial mill towns had some kind of escape 'route' to a nearby rural retreat. Many Bradfordians looked to the Aire Valley and the sylvan beauties of Shipley Glen or the breezy heights of Dick Hudsons and Baildon Moor. Some walked collectively on Whitsunday; some walked competitively on the first Bradford Walk in 1903 but the majority struck out on their own or with their immediate family and found tranquility, like the family in the photograph, on some moorland top.

'We were all great walkers then, with the best walking country in the world so close; before the motor-car had taken possession of England; when what are now motoring roads, bristling with signs and warnings, were still moorland tracks. I knew men who walked forty miles or so every fine Sunday, swinging rather stiffly from the hips, the upper body bent forward a little, in a kind of long lurch that looks ungainly, in a drovers' and shepherds' style, but devours the upland miles unwearyingly, almost without effort until the end of the day.'

Margin Released (1962)

Farmers saw the commercial opportunities in catering for the thousands who rambled and walked the countryside at weekends and Bank Holidays. Everywhere farmhouses began to offer refreshment and some became quite famous for their 'am 'n' egg teas.

'In those days the farmhouses would give you a sevenpenny tea, and there was always more on the table than you could eat. Everybody was knowledgeable about the Dales and their walks, and would spend hours discussing the minutest details of them. You caught the fever when you were quite young, and it never left you. However small and dark your office or warehouse was, somewhere inside your head the high moors were glowing, the curlews were crying, and there blew a wind as salt as if it came straight from the middle of the Atlantic.'

English Journey *(1984)*

At the turn of the century the wealthier artisan or professional person took to renting country cottages for short lets during the summer. These, at Moorside, Baildon match perfectly Priestley's description opposite of the location.

Sunday band concerts during the summer were a recreational highlight of the week for many families. No self-respecting artisan would be seen here in his clogs on a Sunday and the weekday cloth cap image gave way to white collar and stud, best suit and 'billy-cock' hat.

'By 1913, I remember now, I might or might not condescend to make an appearance at the summer band concerts in Lister Park. This indifference would have been unimaginable to me in 1911, when only rain that never looked like stopping could have kept me away. To be somewhere else actually preferring the mere crumbs of existence when the band would be playing in Lister Park—no, I could not have dreamt it of myself two years earlier.'

Margin Released (1962)

'In those days there were well-built stone cottages, within sight of Broad-stone Moor, to be rented for a shilling or eighteenpence a week, and all manner of folk in Bruddersford, cheerfully doing without all conveniences, did rent them. the Alingtons had two adjoining cottages, stout as little fortresses and with hardly more window space, in a village called Bulsden, on the edge of Broadstone Moor.

The Alington cottages were the middle ones of a row of six in a little hollow between Bulsden and the moor. They looked out on to a smooth green, beyond which the rocky moorland rose sharply. We descended from the road to the green . . .'

Bright Day (1946)

Photographs of two young Bradford men. Firstly Pratt's camera catches a 1914 newsboy at the junction of Leeds Road and Vicar Lane. In the second photograph, a youthful Priestley (aged 20) in the uniform of the 10th Duke of Wellington's regiment, shortly before he left Bradford for training at Halifax in 1914.

'In August 1914, when the newsboys were running and shouting every day and all day, I was alone in the house, my family being at the seaside. I waited until they came back before I enlisted, in early September. years later, I often asked myself why I had joined the Army. The usual explanations were no good. I was not hot with patriotic feeling; I did not believe that Britain was in any real danger. I was sorry for 'gallant little Belgium' but did not feel she was waiting for me to rescue her. The legend of Kitchener, who pointed at us from every hoarding, had never captured me. I was not under any pressure from public opinion, which had not got to work on young men as early as that; the white feathers came later. I was not carried to the recruiting office in a herd of chumps, nobody thinking, everybody half-plastered; I went alone.'

Margin Released (1962)

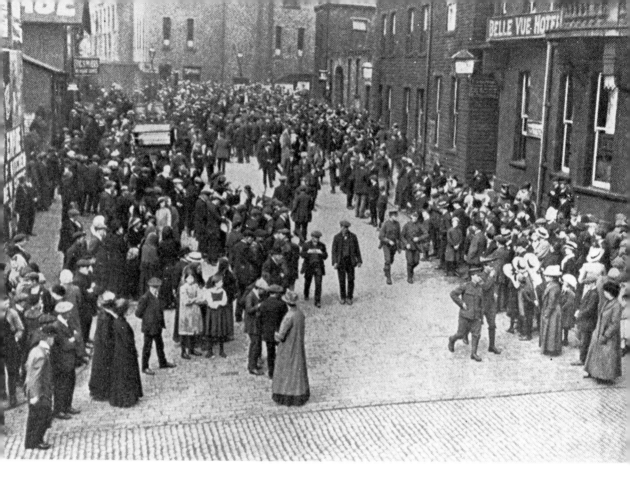

The Sixth Battalion West Yorkshire Regiment was mobilised August 4th, 1914. Four days later a thousand local men had responded to fight for 'King and country'. As E635 they were assembled here at Belle Vue Barracks.

'So early in September, I joined, like a chump, the infantry—to be precise, the Duke of Wellington's West Riding Regiment, known in some circles as 'The Havercake Lads' in others as the 'Dirty Dukes'...'

Margin Released *(1962)*

A week later the battalion left the barracks at the crack of dawn. Their early morning march along Manningham Lane to the Midland Railway station was watched by solitary shift workers; there was no cheering, no acclaim as the Bradford 'Pals' Battalion marched off to the holocaust of the Western front. The Bradford Pals, including men of Priestley's boyhood, companions and school friends, were slaughtered on the Somme in July 1916.

'there was a gang of us there, lads who played football together, went 'chumping', played tin-can-squat round the half built houses, climbed and larked about on the builder's timber stacks, exchanged penny dreadfuls and sometimes made plans for an adventurous future. If those plans had been more sensible, they would still have been futile; for out of this group, there are only two of us left alive...

There are great gaps in my acquaintance now; and I find it difficult to swop reminiscences of boyhood. "The men who were boys when I was a boy," the poet chants; but the men who were boys when I was a boy are dead. Indeed, they never even grew to be men. They were slaughtered in youth; and the parents of them have gone lonely, the girls they would have married have grown grey in spinsterhood, and the work they would have done has remained undone.'

English Journey (1984)

J. B. Priestley's Yorkshire

MANY OF J. B. Priestley's writings on Yorkshire are almost buried among his vast literary output. Some in fact are surprisingly little known. The following is a selected list in chronological order; it makes no claim to be comprehensive:

"Round the Hearth" (***Bradford Pioneer***, 1913)
(Series of weekly articles, initialled J. B. P., running from 24th January to 10th October. "Now the first regular writing I ever did, as a youth in my teens, was for this same ***Bradford Pioneer***. I wrote a weekly feature called 'Round the Hearth', in which, as I knew nothing, I wrote about everything. I was not paid anything, but occasionally received a free pass to a theatre or music-hall.")

"Musings of an Idle Fellow" (***Yorkshire Observer***, 1919)
(Weekly articles, under the pen-name "Peter of Pomfret", running from 21st May to 6th August. Further general articles were contributed on a weekly basis until 22nd October, and from 27th April 1920 to 12th January 1921, latterly initialled J. B. P.)

"A Wayfarer goes to Wensleydale" (***Yorkshire Observer***, 23rd May 1919)
"A Wayfarer in Wensleydale" (***Yorkshire Observer***, 30th May 1919)
(J. B.'s first published writing on the Yorkshire Dales. "The first thing I did after being demobilised in the spring of 1919 was to persuade the editor of the ***Yorkshire Observer*** that he needed some articles by me on the Yorkshire Dales. He paid me a guinea a piece, but you could buy a lot of beer and ham-and-eggs and cut plug for a guinea then.")

"Reminiscences" (***Belle Vue Boys School Magazine***, 1927)
"Schooldays" (***Yorkshire Observer***, 11th February 1928 and 4th November 1947)
"Yorkshire and Christmas: Where the Festive Season is really Festive" (***Yorkshire Post***, 22nd December 1928)

The Good Companions (Heinemann, 1929)
(J. B.'s best-selling, 250,000-word novel set in a Bradford thinly disguised as Bruddersford.)

"Bradford" (***The Heaton Review***, 1931)
(Brief pen portrait of 1930's Bradford in which J. B. refers to the town as "a lost world". He laments: "I could write a huge book on the Bradford I knew, but a short article, a sketch, an impression – why the notion is absurd." Sadly, the "huge book" was never written.)

English Journey (Heinemann, 1934; Jubilee Edition with 80 period photographs, 1984)

(A watershed in travel books, looking at contemporary life – warts and all – as opposed to the then fashion of concentrating on the romantic and glamorous. The chapter "To the West Riding" includes a lengthy section on Bradford, which J. B. used as a base during his 1933 Journey for visiting many other parts of the Riding including the Dales. "I took a day's holiday from my ***English Journey***, mostly spent grumpily moving from one dismal hole to the next, to revisit Wharfedale.")

Four-in-Hand (Heinemann, 1934)

(Features a visit to Dick Hudson's, the pub above Eldwick forming "the most familiar gateway to the moors".)

The Beauty of Britain (Batsford, 1935)

(Introduction by J. B. with references to the Yorkshire Dales – "A day's walk among them will give you almost everything fit to be seen on this earth.")

They Walk in the City (Heinemann, 1936)
(Novel, partly set in "Haliford" – Halifax)

Midnight on the Desert: A Chapter of Autobiography (Heinemann, 1937)

When We are Married: A Yorkshire Farcical Comedy (Heinemann, 1938)
(One of J. B.'s favourite plays – a characterful assessment of West Riding family life in the lingering Edwardian twilight.)

Rain upon Godshill: A Further Chapter of Autobiography (Heinemann, 1939)

Bright Day (Heinemann, 1945)
(Again set in Bruddersford. Along with ***Lost Empires*** and ***The Image Men***, widely considered to be one of J. B.'s best novels.)

"Born and Bred in Bradford" (***The Listener***, 27th December 1945)
(Article later reprinted in ***The Radio Listener's Week-End Book*** (Odhams, 1950).)

Article on Bradford (***Telegraph & Argus***, 17th June 1946)

"Bradford when I was Young" (***Yorkshire Observer***, 19th December 1946)
(Article abridged from J. B.'s Preface to ***Socialism over Sixty Years – the Life of Jowett of Bradford*** (Allen & Unwin, 1946).)

"Bruddersford Revisited"(***The Listener***, 7th June 1951)

The Other Place (Heinemann, 1953)

(Makes a brief reference to Hubberholme – "one of the smallest and pleasantest places in the world".)

The Yorkshire Story (Yorkshire Insurance Company, 1954)

(Introduction by J. B.)

"Why I regret the closing of Bradford's Giant-Pie Shop" (*Yorkshire Observer*, 20th June 1955)

"The Bradford Schoolmaster" (*The Listener*, 23rd July 1959)

Margin Released (Heinemann, 1962)

(Reminiscent work, with chapter "The Swan Arcadian" recalling the Bradford of 1910-14.)

"A Walk in the Park" (*Sunday Times Magazine*, 4th October 1964)

(J. B. "goes back to the Dales he has known for more than half a century".)

Lost Empires (Heinemann, 1965)

(Novel about the early music and variety halls, drawing on J. B.'s experiences in Bradford before 1914 when he was a frequent visitor to the Palace Theatre and the Empire.)

Article on the Bradford wool office in which J. B. worked for a season (*The Clerk*, 1966)

"Wuthering Heights to Arcadia in a Sharp Two-Hour Walk" (*Life International*, 7th March 1966)

(Article in premier American magazine commenting wittily on the less obvious facets of Dales landscape and life. Fully illustrated with photographs and reproductions of some of J. B.'s paintings.)

"Priestley's Bradford" (*Telegraph & Argus*, 16th July 1968)

(Article in newspaper's Centenary supplement.)

"Conifers in the Yorkshire Dales" (*The Times*, 4th march 1970)

(Letter protesting at coniferous afforestation in upper Langstrothdale – "so destroying its stark magnificence".)

"Bradford that I knew Best" (*Telegraph & Argus*, 7th September 1973)

The Essential West Riding: Its Character in Words and Pictures (E. P., 1975)
(Foreword by J. B.)

* * *

An annotated bibliography of all the writings of J. B. Priestley has been compiled by A. E. Day and was published in a limited edition by Ian Hodgkins & Co in 1980.